BATTERSEA PARK

An illustrated history

PUBLISHED BY
THE FRIENDS OF BATTERSEA PARK

First published in Great Britain in 1993 by
The Friends of Battersea Park,
Battersea Park, London SW11 4NJ

ISBN 0-9520981-0-5

Printed in Great Britain by Battley Brothers, London SW4

ABOVE: The original timber bridge and fountain in the Ladies' Pond.

COVER CAPTIONS

FRONT: Beside the lake in Edwardian times.
BACK: The cricket pitch in the 1920s and (below) the Festival of Britain funfair in 1951.

ACKNOWLEDGMENTS

The Friends of Battersea Park wish to express their sincere gratitude to the following: the authors of the five chapters in this book – Martyn Goff, Alex MacCormick, Jasmine Mitchell and Tom Pocock; Jackie McCabe, Principal Landscape Officer, Wandsworth Borough Council, on whose extensive research both the permanent audio-visual display in Battersea Park Pump House and much of this book is based; Anthony Leavey for research material; Anthony Shaw of Wandsworth Local History Library; the publisher and designer, Frank Phillips; the editor, Alex MacCormick; Martyn Goff and National Book Trust for help in sales and promotion; Paul Faulkner for help with sales; the printers, Battley Brothers; and last, but far from least, Lance Garrett, David Parker, John Pitt and their colleagues at Wandsworth Borough Council, whose financial support and encouragement made publication of this book possible.

PICTURE CREDITS

Grateful acknowledgement is made to the following for kind permission to reproduce illustrations: **Irene Lissman**, p. 2. **Battersea District Library**, three cover pictures, pp 4, 8, 11, 13 (below), 16, 17, 20, 22, (above left), 23, 24, 26, 27, 28 (both), 30 (below), 33, 37, 40, 42 (both), 43, 45 (both), 46, 47, 48 (above), 49, 50, 52, 54, 56 (above), 59, 60 (above), 62, 65, 68 (illus. E. W. Fenton), 71 (photo L. & M. Taylor), 74, 75 (photo L. & M. Taylor), 76 (photo Raphael Tuck), 77 (photo L. & M. Taylor), 78 (photo Charles Skilton Ltd), 79 (photos above L. & M. Taylor, below Valentin & Son), 82 (left, photo D. Barlishie). **Private Collection**, p. 6. **Public Records Office**, Kew, pp 10, 22 (below), 66, 72. **Michael Bryan**, pp. 13, 18, 19, 25. **British Architectural Library/RIBA**, p. 22 (above right). **Descendants of Thomas Allom**, p. 25. **Cassell, Peter & Galpin** (*Old and New London* by W. Thornbury), pp. 29, 31. **Ruth Forrest**, p. 30 (top). **Royal Botanic Gardens, Kew**, p. 35. **Estate of the late Cyril Ray**, p. 38. **Ron Elam's Local Yesterdays**, pp 48 (below), 52, 56 (below), 57, 60 (below), 63 (left). **Frank Phillips**, p.58. **Jackie McCabe**, p. 63 (right). **Wandsworth Museum**, p. 64. **Corporation of London, Greater London Records Office**, p. 81. **Peter Dunant**, p. 82 (right). While every effort has been made to trace copyright holders, any errors or omissions will gladly be rectified in the next edition.

The entrance to Battersea Park near Chelsea Bridge in the early 1900s.

CONTENTS

The Boating Pond, Battersea Park painted in 1870 by Walter Greaves (1846-1930). Walter's father, a boat-builder and Thames waterman, had been Turner's boatman in the old painter's final Chelsea days. Walter too worked in the family boatyard, where the skiffs for hire on the lake were built. He was an enthusiastic artist even before he came under the influence of the painter James Whistler, who befriended him in 1860.

INTRODUCTION

The aim of this volume is to inform and amuse, but in no way does it pretend to be an encyclopaedia. Some of the history of Battersea Fields is sketched in the first chapter, whilst the subsequent four recall more fully many of the highlights in the creation and evolution of the park itself.

The number and choice of illustrations were necessarily constrained by space, but we hope they will bring vividly to life diverse aspects of the park's development in the course of the past 150 years or so.

Above all, however, this book stands as a modest tribute to the splendid achievements of the superintendents/park managers, their staff and all those, past and present, who have laboured lovingly to care for Battersea Park.

The Friends of Battersea Park,
Battersea Park SW11 4NJ,
London.

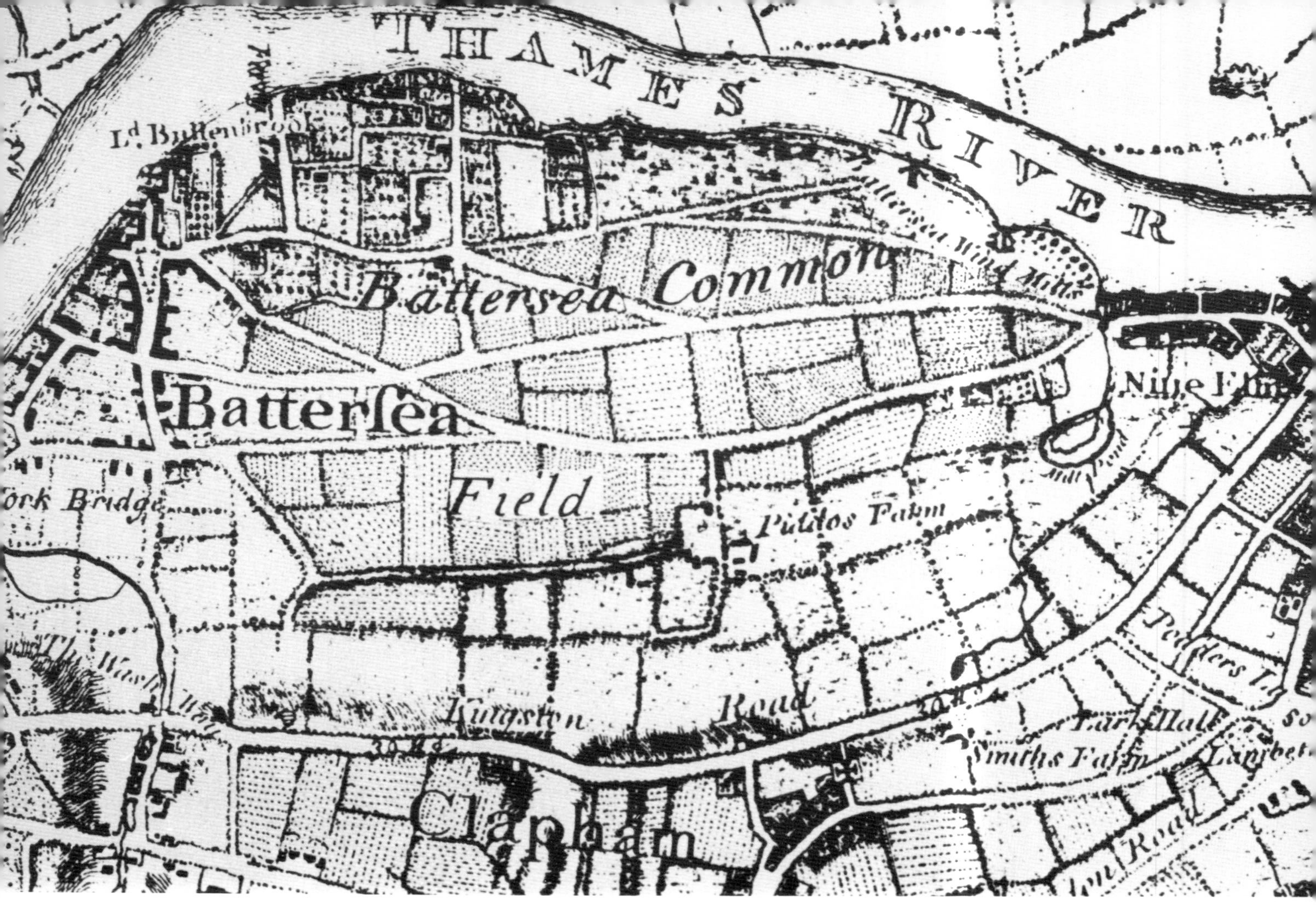

Battersea Fields and Common with their marshlands
and riverside windmills.

BEFORE THE PARK

'Here there was a place out of Hell that surpassed Sodom and Gomorrah in ungodliness and abomination,' declared a former city missionary of Battersea Fields in the early nineteenth century. Not a few local people may feel much the same on occasions of particularly frenzied activity in Battersea Park today, but, although not uneventful, most of the area's history has not been so outrageous.

Did Julius Caesar's Roman legions ford the Thames in the vicinity of what is now Battersea Park? It seems entirely possible. But the first recorded mention of Battersea does not occur until the Dark Ages of the seventh century, when King Caedwalla of Wessex granted the manor of Batrices Ege (Badric's or Marshy Island) to Eorienweald, Bishop of London (675-693), for religious purposes, possibly for use by the nunnery at Barking, where his sister Ethelburga was the first abbess.

The small settlement on a gravel island and its surrounding marshlands were bounded to the south by Hidaburn stream (Falcon Brook), which debouched into the Thames north of where York House now is. The stream was later connected in the region of present-day Falcon Road to the Ditch of Bradmede, a partly man-made water course later known less appealingly as

Heath Wall Sewer. This ran not far north of and parallel to a raised road (now Wandsworth Road) running from Wandleswurth to Lambehide (Lambeth) and thence into London. Battersea Park Road follows approximately the route of what was once the 'Foote Path from Battersea [Village] to London' via Nine Elms.

Today we are accustomed to measuring areas in acres, yards or metres, but in William the Conqueror's time, when he commissioned the *Domesday Book* to be compiled (1085-6), land was commonly measured in Saxon 'hides'. In the case of Battersea, recent research indicates that 1 hide = 47½ acres, sufficient in theory to support one family; the total recorded population of Battersea at the time of the following extract from the *Domesday Book* was sixty-nine:

THE LAND OF THE CHURCH OF WESTMINSTER In Brixton Hundred

- St Peter of Westminster holds Battersea. Earl [King] Harold held it. It was then assessed at 72 hides, and now at 18 hides. There is land . . . In demesne [land belonging to the manor] are 3 ploughs; and 45 villans [serfs] and 16 bordars [tenants] with 14 ploughs. There are 8 slaves, and 7 mills rendering £42 9s. 8d, or wheat to the same value, and 82 acres of meadow, and woodland for 50 pigs as pannage [swine fodder]; and in Southwark 1 bordar paying 12d. From the toll of Wandsworth, £6. From a villan having 10 pigs, 1 pig; if less, he gives nothing.

A knight holds 4 hides of the land of this manor. His livestock is reckoned above with the other.

The whole was worth TRE £80; and afterwards £30; now £75 9s. 8d. King William [I, the Conqueror] gave this manor to St Peter's in exchange for Windsor [Berks].

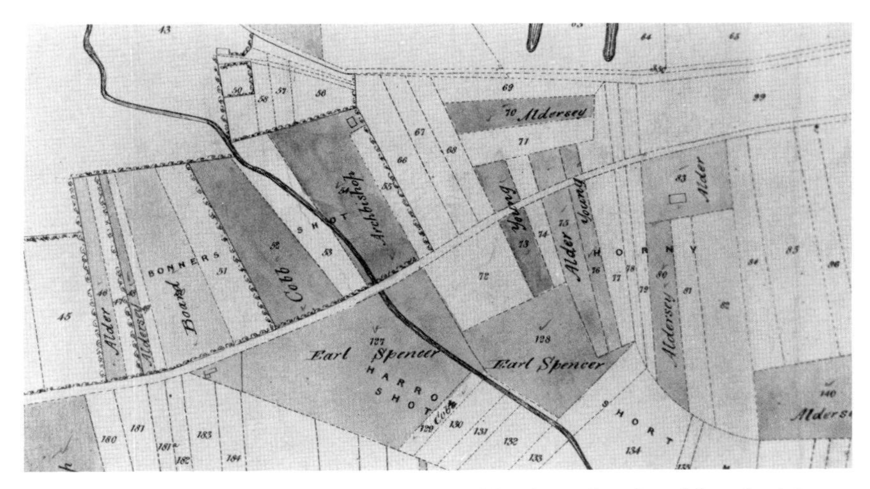

Strip fields in Battersea were owned by hundreds of freeholders including Earl Spencer

• The Count of Mortain holds of the land of this manor 1½ hides, which belonged to it TRE, and for some time afterwards. Gilbert the priest holds 3 hides; they had been [held] in the same way. The Bishop of Lisieux [holds] 2 hides of which the church was seised in the time of King William; and afterwards the Bishop of Bayeux disseised it. The Abbot of Chertsey holds 1 hide, . . . which the reeve [steward] of this vill[age], on account of some enmity, took away from this manor and put it in Chertsey.

During the medieval times much of the open land and marsh which came to be known as Battersea Fields (approximately the area north of Lavender Hill up to the Thames and between Battersea Village on the west and beyond Chelsea Bridge towards Nine Elms on the east) was farmed in a patchwork of strips, each owned by a separate person or family. The pattern of strip farming

The Red House
Pigeon Shooting Grounds
Gough House
Chelsea College
New Chelsea Water Works

LEFT: Part of the 1828 panorama of the Thames by Samuel Leigh.
TOP: *View of Old Battersea Bridge from the South-West*, 1885, by H. R. Cauty.
ABOVE: The river bank near the Red House early in the nineteenth century.

and the boggy land which ran down to the Thames remained almost unchanged until 1846, when there were as many as 367 individual farm plots, the largest covering 6 acres and the smallest only a few square yards. Little wonder then that once the powers that be eventually decided to buy up Battersea Fields to create a park, it took seven years to purchase all the relevant plots.

Here, in this seemingly timeless medieval setting, Colonel Blood in 1671 hid in the reeds intending to shoot King Charles II whilst he bathed in the river, but, as the Colonel confessed at his subsequent trial for audaciously attempting to steal the Crown Jewels, his arm 'was checked by an awe of majesty'. Here, too, was fought one of the most famous pistol duels of Georgian times.

At sunrise on 21 March 1829 the Prime Minister – no less a figure than the Duke of Wellington, the redoubtable 'Iron Duke' who vanquished Napoleon's troops at the Battle of Waterloo in 1815 – arranged to fight a political critic, the Earl of Winchilsea. The subject of their quarrel was a letter to the *Standard* newspaper. Wellington, then aged fifty-one, had been in office only a year, but an Irish crisis had already arisen. To force essential legislation through Parliament he had to shift his position, and his enemies were quick to react. (How familiar this all sounds even today.) One of these opponents, the quarrelsome Earl, published a letter accusing the Prime Minister of double dealing.

Over the next four days there ensued an exchange of angry notes, which culminated in Wellington issuing a challenge: 'I now call upon your lordship to give me that satisfaction for your conduct which a gentleman has a right to require, and which a gentleman never refuses to give [ie to fight a duel].'

Dr Hume, who recorded the events in his journal, was summoned by

Wellington's second, Sir Henry Hardinge, before dawn on 21 March to accompany him to an affair of honour between 'persons of rank and consequence' – no mention being made of the protagonists' names. Wellington and Hardinge set off on horseback from the Duke's home, Apsley House at Hyde Park Corner. The unsuspecting Doctor followed some way behind in a carriage as they went along King's Road, past the old houses of Cheyne Walk and over the wooden Battersea Bridge. At the site nominated for the duel – according to author and historian Tom Pocock, what is nowadays the crossroads of old Surrey Lane, Battersea Bridge Road and the western end of Prince of Wales Drive – Wellington spurred his horse up to the astonished Dr Hume and announced, 'Well, I dare say you little expected it was I who wanted you to be here.'

Fortunately for all concerned, the Doctor's medical expertise was not in fact put to the test. The Duke, firing first, missed the Earl, who then shot into the air and offered his apologies. Thus one of Britain's most popularly admired prime ministers lived to fight another political day.

For the most part, in the early decades of the 1800s, Battersea Fields were the scene of quietly desperate agricultural activity. Separated from the river by a narrow raised causeway, the fields still comprised low marshes intersected by black streams and ditches where the chief crops were carrots, melons, lavender and the famous local asparagus sold in 'Battersea bunches'. Beyond the fields silent masses toiled in industrial concerns including a pottery, copper works, a lime kiln, chemical works, docks, wharves, riverside windmills and later the railways. On Sundays, however, the area echoed to sounds of as many as 40,000 people indulging in merrymaking and amusement.

'On the Lord's day . . . there have been horses and donkey racing, walking matches, flying boats, flying horses, roundabouts, fortune-tellers, and gamblers

Contemporary cartoon of the duel between
the Duke of Wellington (left) and
the Earl of Winchilsea in 1829.

of every description, drinking booths, stalls, hawkers and vendors,' lamented a pious contemporary.

Here, on the fields and marshes, the local gentry came to shoot live pigeons (purchased at fifteen shillings a dozen), starlings (four shillings a dozen) and sparrows (two shillings a dozen). Afterwards they repaired to mix with the

An encounter near the
Red House tavern.

working-class folk at temporary drinking booths scattered along the river bank and in the notoriously bawdy Red House tavern often patronised by Charles Dickens. In the centre of the hostelry's garden was a fish pond and around it seven arbours adorned with paintings and flowering plants; in each of these alcoves was a table for twelve, lit at night by glowing oil lamps – a congenial

ABOVE: *The Old Red House with a Livery Company Barge on the River* by Walter Greaves.
OPPOSITE: *View of the Old Red House, Battersea,* 1850, by C. H. Norris.

venue for a bit of tipsy hanky-panky.

Exciting as this may sound to modern readers, at the time the Vicar of St Mary's in Battersea, the Rev. Robert Eden, was deeply concerned about the moral and physical health of his parishioners, especially the working-class ones, many of whose families lived in dreadfully squalid conditions, their poverty aggravated by drink, gambling and the noxious vapours of the marshes. So this enterprising man prepared his own plan for a 315-acre park and wrote to the Prime Minister; he advised the Royal Commission for Metropolitan Works that 'many of these people would become orderly if pain were taken to provide for them healthful recreation [and by providing a park the Commissioners] will promote social and domestic happiness; they will implant feelings which are now deadened by dirt, by drink and by discomfort.'

In the face of mounting criticism and the growing unruliness of the huge crowds in Battersea Fields, dramatic changes to the area became inevitable.

The opening of the Subtropical Garden in 1863, with its outdoor display of palms and other tender exotics resulted in the park rivalling even Kew Gardens in nationwide acclaim and fame

CREATION OF THE PARK

We tend to associate Thomas Cubitt with Belgravia and Mayfair, and to think of him as an entrepreneurial builder who nowadays we would call 'a developer'. But it was in large part to Cubitt that we owe the transformation of the notorious Battersea Fields into the salubrious Battersea Park.

In 1843 Cubitt and the local vicar, the Honourable Reverend Robert Eden, gave evidence to Queen Victoria's Commission for Improving the Metropolis. Sir James Pennethorne, one of the architects who competed to design the Albert Memorial – and lost to Norman Scott – investigated Cubitt's plea. At one point in the questioning Cubitt was asked: 'Do you include in the term "amusement" the power of healthful enjoyment in baths to be constructed?'

To which he replied: 'No ground is better calculated for the formation of baths than the ground of Battersea Fields, for at high water the baths can be filled to any requisite height, and emptied at low water. The water can be changed at every tide.'

Then came a supplementary question: 'And that such baths might be erected in the same general locality with the park?'

'Unquestionably so, for they might be planted out from the public gaze.

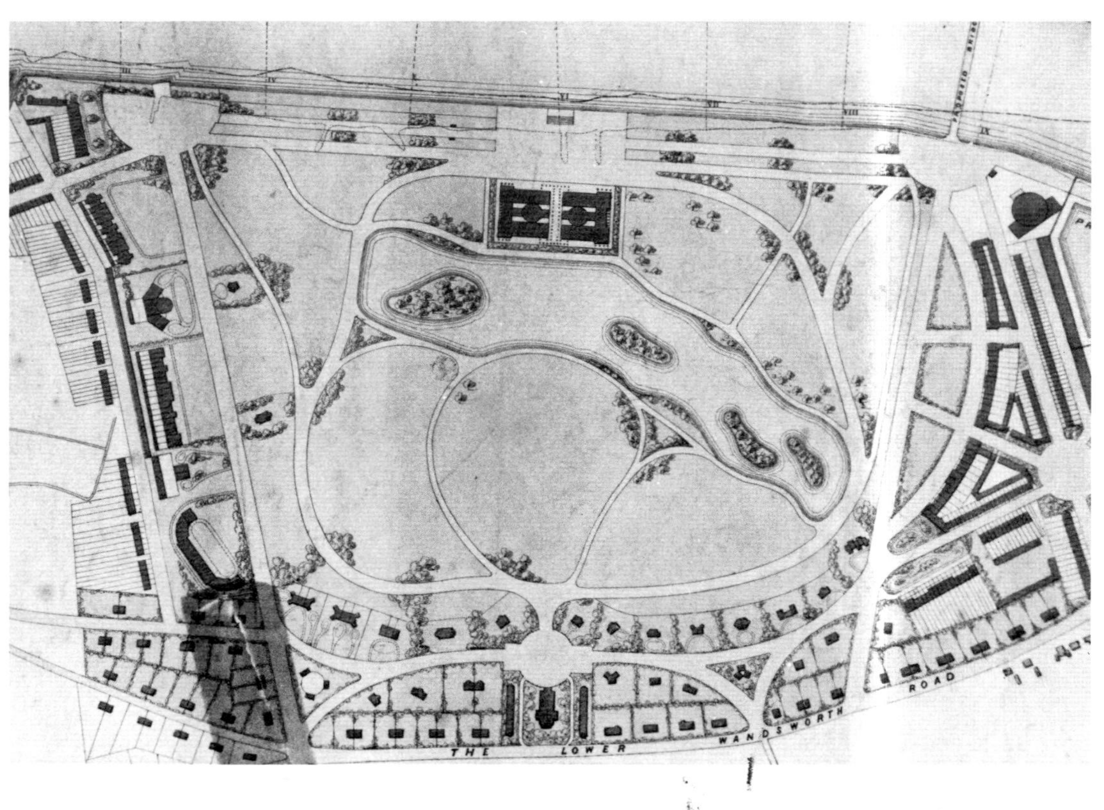
THE LOWER WANDSWORTH ROAD

Baths are essentially necessary, for owing to the frequent passage of steam boats, it is impossible for working men as formerly to bathe in the river. Decency forbids it, and the river is also a very dangerous place for persons who cannot swim.'

Cubitt's motives for urging the purchase of the land and lay-out of the Park have been questioned. Not only was he a developer, but his original scheme gave 200 acres to the Park and over a 100 for the building of villas. But in fact

ABOVE: A view south-east across the lake to Albert Palace, which encompassed (left to right) an exhibition hall, concert hall, conservatory, aviary and hippodrome.
OPPOSITE TOP LEFT: Thomas Cubitt.
OPPOSITE TOP RIGHT: James Pennethorne (1801-1871).
OPPOSITE BELOW: Pennethorne's original 1845 plan for the park and new buildings around it was later greatly modified.

ABOVE: An engraved view of 1858 showing newly created and planted mounds and winding paths. RIGHT: *Chelsea Suspension Bridge, c.* 1852, by Thomas Allom.

he was a notably humane individual. His daily contact with hundreds of poor building labourers had taught him about their deprivations in terms of everyday living standards. That said, Cubitt had been buying parcels of land in Battersea Fields from 1839 to 1841, both from the existing tenants and from Earl Spencer.

On 8 October 1845 an application was made to Parliament for a bill to form and make a Royal Park containing 330 acres. The Act was passed in 1846; and £200,000 was promised for the purchase of the land. Then, as now, governments failed to keep their promises. Benjamin Disraeli, Chancellor of the Exchequer in 1852, would have none of it: 'Of all the speculations man ever

engaged in, no speculation was as absurd as that of Battersea Park. The persons who undertook the enterprise were totally ignorant of all the circumstances with which they had to deal.' Cubitt, however, called the Chancellor's bluff: he offered to buy the park at cost, an offer firmly rejected in May 1853.

On 6 December of that year there was the first sale of building materials by order of the Honourable Commissioners of Her Majesty's Work and Buildings, comprising the Red House tavern, White Mill and cottage adjoining, and consisting of about 200,000 Capital Stock bricks.

Meanwhile, the land was being cleared of more animate materials. 'On and after 9 May 1852 all PERSONS found trespassing in BATTERSEA FIELDS with Horses, Donkeys, Cockshies, Barrows on a Sunday will be taken into custody.'

In 1858 Queen Victoria was finally able to declare Battersea Park, and the newly built Chelsea Bridge, open; and four years later the Royal Agricultural

The Royal Agricultural Society Show, July 1862.

Show was held there – the nearest it has ever come to the centre of the capital.

It remains to add that the bill for the 316 acres came to £230,687 16s. 4d, of which the Park was allocated 200 acres, while a further £80,000 was spent on laying it out – a task so brilliantly achieved that, some years later, a magazine was to comment: ' In the morning the Park presents a scene of gaiety and brightness which would lead one to imagine that a bit of Paris and its Bois de Boulogne had been transferred to our sombre city.'

In 1860 the ornamental lake was excavated and designed with considerable

In the Swiss cattle shed at the show.

bravura; four years later came the renowned Subtropical Garden. The grounds round the lake were then decorated with the remarkable rockworks devised by James Pulham, screening off the new railway lines being part of the intention behind this. A description quoted in a late nineteenth-century book, *Old and New London* by Edward Walford, is relevant:

> The Avenue is one of the principal features and forms the chief promenade of the Park. The trees are English Elms. To appreciate Battersea Park it must

TOP: Central Avenue, originally of elms, was lined with railings and shrubs, *c.*1906.
ABOVE: Gibson's innovative mixing of exotic foliage plants with bedding plants in the Subtropical Garden – seen here in 1910 – was widely copied.
OPPOSITE: The lake edges too were imaginatively planted.

A wide variety of exotic and native plants graced the Cascades and lake margins in Edwardian times.
OPPOSITE: The rockwork of the Cascades, constructed between 1866 and 1870, was designed by James Pulham.

not be approached in a hurry. Its numerous beauties are worth much more than a bird's eye view . . . But the palm trees we speak of do not flourish in the more aristocratic parks of the metropolis – they have found a home in Battersea Park, the access to which is easy in all directions. Steamers ply to it at all hours of the day; but we prefer to approach it from quaint old Chelsea and on a bright Sunday in Summer.

Aristocratic or not, the main plan, which succeeded Pennethorne's original one of 1845, was largely geometrical. The Park was divided into four quarters, with the east-west axis formed by a half-mile long avenue forty feet wide, while the north-south axis has a straight path. At the junction of these paths is placed a central circular space, while the north-south axis terminated in semi-circular paths and spaces next to the riverside café (where the Pagoda now stands). Each corner of this huge rectangle has an entrance, with another at the end of the north-south axis. The lake was decorated with islands and promontories and placed in the south-east corner.

While the park in its early days was more of a botanical garden than a wild park, the open grass areas looked more like rural fields than today's sports grounds. The gardenesque style so produced derived in part from Edward Kemp's *How to Lay Out a Garden* with its first principles described by Loudon in *Remarks on the Laying Out of Public Gardens and Promenades* (1835) as a recognition of gardening as a fine art. This unified work of art consists of one main walk with 'a series of minor episodial walks to display the particular scenes in detail'. Variety is achieved by 'increasing the inequalities of surface; by varying the views along that walk; by concealing the boundary everywhere except on the river side and at the principal entrance; and, above all, by planting the most extensive collection of trees and shrubs.'

Although little still survives of the original planting, evidence of Kemp's recommendations remains:

Serpentine or wavy lines may be regarded as the characteristic features of

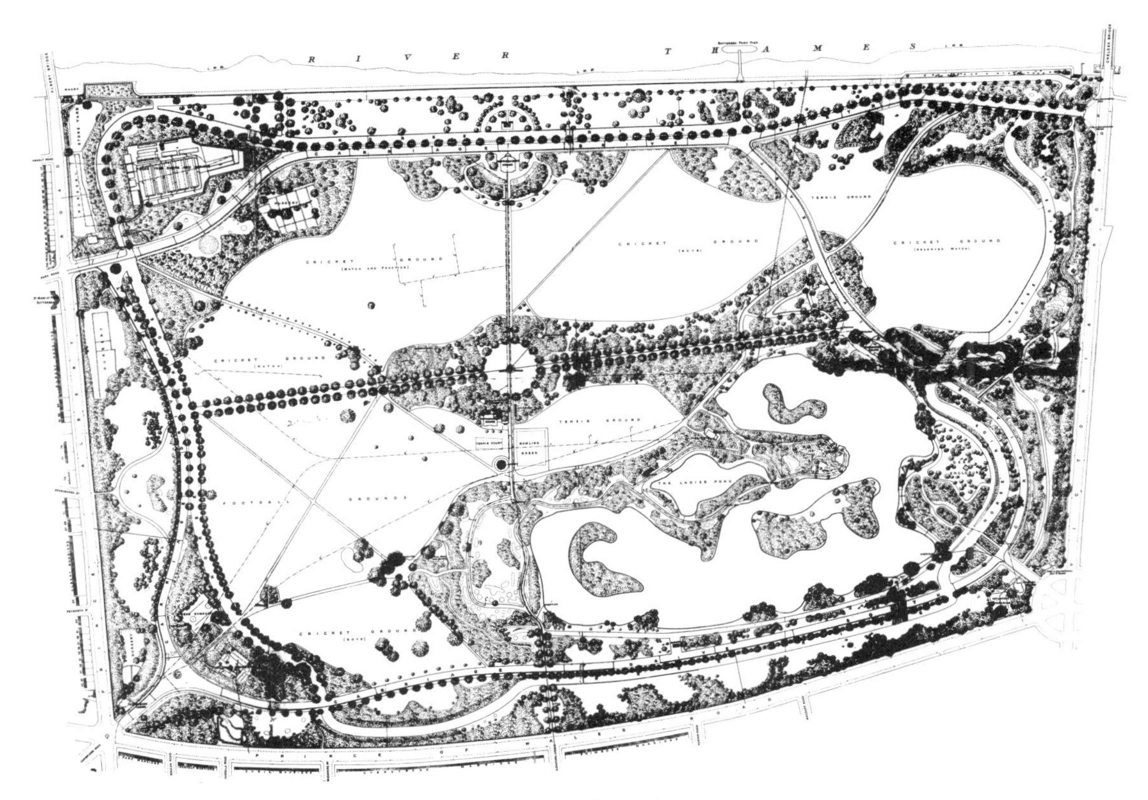

Battersea Park in 1888.

the mixed style. Its object is beauty of line and general variety. Roundness, smoothness, freedom of angularity, and grace rather than dignity . . . It is a blending of art and nature, combining the vagaries of one with the regularity of the other.

The original detailed plan was drawn up by James Pennethorne. Educated by John Nash and then, later, working with Charles Pugin, he had travelled widely on the Continent and worked on St James's Park and the East and West Villages on the border of Regent's Park. Regent's Park was in many ways his model, though the grand villas and terraces were not to be copied in Battersea; the arrival of the railway precluded this on the east (Nine Elms) side, while mansion blocks eventually lined the south.

Although we think of using commercial developments to finance public ones as a modern idea, this was precisely what was in the minds of the Commissioners of Woods and Forests. If, as intended, the public roads, Chelsea and Albert Bridges had come first, then the self-financing might have been achieved through posh housing. As it was, the park was completed first. The Commissioners had been authorised to borrow £120,000 for the construction and a further £80,000 for Chelsea Bridge, but the Public Works Loan Commissioners soon ran out of money.

Money was not the only problem. Records show that:

> The low level of the Park may be disguised and the beauty and appearance of the Park greatly increased if time is allowed for the deposit of earth to raise the levels in many parts.
>
> 120 men are employed on raising and forming an esplanade by the river the whole length of the Park, 120 feet broad and four feet above the Trinity high water.

John Gibson became Superintendent of Battersea Park in 1856. He had originally been apprenticed to Joseph Paxton and then became head gardener to the Duke of Devonshire. He had also worked with Pennethorne before.

John Gibson (1815-1875),
the park's first Superintendent.

By now there had been much overspending, and Pennethorne's explanations were not accepted. After twelve years' work Gibson found that 'as regards landscape effects, the Park can scarcely be said to possess any beyond those which are usually associated with a flat surface.' He goes on:

> The very unfavourable nature of the locality for the purpose . . . so much labour and an incredible quantity of three quarters of a million cubic yards of material brought in having been required to raise marshy parts to dry level to suit the levels given by the New Bridge [Chelsea].

It took Gibson fourteen years to complete his plan. Money apart, one detail shows why: 'Plantations comprise 20 acres with 44,058 trees and shrubs suitable for the locality plus several thousand American trees from the Royal Gardens at Kew.'

For the river front embankment Gibson planted 'groups of ornamental trees, including acers, alders, poplars, elms, ash thorns, pyrus and planes,' while the shrub planting contained 'dwarf growing types of rhododendrons, berberis aquifolia, darwinii, japonica, dulcas, and impetunifolia, cotoneaster microphylia, juniperus prostrata and tamariscifolia.'

Nearly twenty years later the *Gardener's Magazine* described other plantings which had been planned and carried out since 1865:

> Between the horse and carriage drive there had been planted thirty-three planes measuring thirteen inches in circumference, and thirty-three chesnuts, measuring nine inches . . . From the south gate to the west gate there had been planted thirty planes and thirty gleditsias by the side of the path.

Gibson's colourful carpet bedding proved controversial at the time, but was later much imitated and, indeed, can still be seen in many places today.

The *Gardener's Chronicle* of 1864 was more critical of another aspect of the park's bedding:

> The individual whose soul is charmed by long lines of colour this, and succeeded by long lines of colour that, and who gloats over the absence of verdure or leaf beauty may go there and be twice blessed, for Mr Gibson had catered for his taste most extensively. Should the misanthropic stroller wish to call up such associates as could be derived from the sight of some great undertaker's black plumes, he need not despair, for behold, in vast lines, Perilla is there.

The same magazine describes Gibson's introduction of bedding involving the use of low ground cover plants, making a uniform surface like a carpet:

A Victorian Afternoon on the riverside promenade depicted by James Aumonier before the embankment was built.

It hardly seems possible at first to realise that one is looking upon a group of living plants, so strange and unfamiliar do their forms appear in this new association. Let the reader picture to himself a circular raised bed of moderate diameter, 5 or 6 feet perhaps, having a large plant of *Echeveria metallica* in its centre, and six smaller ones standing at a little distance around it. Then, close to the central plant, and fitted beneath its leaves, a ring of stemmed plants of *sempieriovum arboreum*, other plants of which again alternate with the smaller echeverias, but stand a little nearer the circumference.

Before long, parks and gardens all over England were experimenting with carpet bedding.

By 1865, 40,000-50,000 people were visiting Battersea Park on Sundays, many of them arriving by steamboat. These incursions meant that various areas of the Park had to be fenced off, including the Subtropical Garden and various areas round the lake. At the same time the boundary was fenced in timber palisade, not as at present in impressive wrought ironwork with gilded tops.

A few years earlier Rosary and Sungate Lodges had been built, while the West Lodge had been pulled down and replaced. In 1861 Simpson & Son built an Italianate Pump and Engine House, intended to draw water from a reservoir, pump it to a cast-iron tank at the top of the tower by means of a steam engine and periodically release it to drive the Cascades. It was never quite successful and serves a better purpose in its 1992 reincarnation as an art gallery.

It had been a long haul from the moment that Cubitt had first proposed his idea to Queen Victoria's Commission for Improving the Metropolis. Money, as so often in England, caused endless delays; the change of concept from a place where the poor could disport themselves on Sundays almost to a second Kew Gardens ensured further hold-ups. And, in the end, as we shall see, Battersea Park reverted more nearly to the earlier intentions, retaining enough of its natural beauty to raise the spirits of poor and rich alike.

THE PARK IN ITS HEYDAY

'Stand up, stand up, man – here comes the Queen!' Ernest Morris, a local worker who had opted for a tranquil sandwich in the open air rather than his usual fourpenny meal in the works canteen, was so startled by this sudden cry from his neighbour on the park bench that, springing to his feet with alacrity, he scattered his precious lunch in the dust. Before him, seated in an open landau, was the formidable, erect figure of Queen Mary (wife of George V and grandmother of the present Queen), accompanied by a lady-in-waiting. As the carriage swept past, Mr Morris recalled the Queen offered him such 'a lovely smile' that, in blushing confusion, he found himself curtseying to Her Majesty instead of bowing. When he later told his workmates and family of this memorable encounter, did he, one wonders, omit this last embarrassing fact? Did they laugh at him?

Looking at Battersea Park now, it is not perhaps easy to visualise it as a place regularly frequented by royalty, yet it was. In its heyday, which stretched from

OPPOSITE: *Cycling in Battersea Park* by E. M. Vickers, 1895.

PERSONS DEPOSITING
PAPER, LITTER OR
RUBBISH OF ANY
SORT IN THIS PARK
WILL BE PROSECUTED

ABOVE: A serpentine path at the turn of the century.
OPPOSITE: Two views of the Old English Garden in its prime.

the last decades of the 1800s through to the outbreak of the First World War in 1914, the park and in particular the Subtropical Garden with its unique collection of outdoor palm trees were widely acclaimed an outstanding success, rivalling even Kew Gardens in national prestige. The heated debates which had accompanied every stage of its planning and creation had faded almost completely by the time London County Council assumed responsibility for running the park in 1889. Some ninety staff were employed in caring for the gardens, avenues, lakes and fountains, and in monitoring the thousands of visitors.

The leisured classes, seeking relief from the smells and congestion of the city, considered it essential to take a daily carriage drive round the park. This became a favourite pastime, combining as it did the pleasure of harmless display – seeing and being seen in one's finery – with the healthy enjoyment of relatively fresh air.

Threading their way through the carriages, hacking horses and walkers there came to be seen an increasing number of cyclists. The advent in the 1880s of rideable bicycles led to this becoming a widely popular activity. Because it was the first park in London to allow cycling on carriage drives, those who had once been enthusiastic horse-riders in Hyde Park forsook their old haunt to join the fashion-conscious in Battersea.

While Mrs Pankhurst and her Suffragettes outraged Edwardian society by such acts as chaining themselves to railings in their struggle to win the right for women to vote, other middle-class ladies caused almost as much horror by casting aside their conventional long skirts and whizzing around on bicycles wearing bloomers. Named after their originator, Mrs Bloomer, these baggy knickerbockers proved ideal for cycling and gave the wearer a measure of freedom she had never before experienced, thus combining practical modesty with a fashion statement.

Other people came to the park, however, to enjoy a growing range of less controversial activities and amenities, the chief focus of which was the lake.

A sunny day early this century and
(BELOW) Edwardian strollers in Central Avenue.

ABOVE: Lakeside planting in its full glory.
OPPOSITE: 'The cycling parade in Battersea Park became one of the sights of the 1895 season' ran the caption to this early photograph.

On balmy summer days breakfast was served at white-clothed tables laid out beneath lakeside trees. Boating had become fashionable during Victorian times and families strolled along paths edged in hooped railings round the lake admiring its marges covered in native grasses, reeds, rushes, giant rhubarb and water irises. Rafts of waterlilies sparkled on the water between the islands. The original rustic bridge over the weir (replaced by the present stone bridge in the 1920s) afforded a fine view of the fountain in the Ladies' Pond.

Stocked with carp, roach, bream and perch, the lake provided good fishing, a sport beloved by many subsequent generations of local anglers. In addition the lake supported a wildfowl population which, in 1886, comprised nine

ABOVE: The rustic bridge with a weir beneath it and the fountain in the Ladies' Pond (originally a reservoir), *c.* 1900.
OPPOSITE: Breakfast by the lake and (BELOW) a typical Sunday scene, *c.* 1910.

white and seven black swans, nineteen geese and ninety-five assorted ducks, looked after by a keeper who, in 1913, received a salary of thirty shillings per week to feed them and monitor their numbers. (How fortunate he was not to have to contend with the later invasion of Canada geese.)

As well as wildfowl, the area round the lake also boasted in Victorian and Edwardian times aviaries containing ornamental pheasants and owls, and the

The joys and
hazzards of skating
in January 1867.

A Sunday bandstand concert in 1905.

deer enclosure (opened in 1896) with its zig-zag path to a viewing area atop a rocky outcrop.

In cold winters, when the ice measured three inches thick and was therefore deemed safe, crowds of excited skaters flocked to the lake. Among them was a Mrs Dixon, who recalls skating there with her parents. There were, she says, some adept local skaters, but 'they were not a patch on the Russian refugees' – presumably White Russians who had fled to England to escape the atrocities of the 1917 Bolshevik Revolution. Keeping an eye on the milling throng were skating attendants equipped with ropes and planks in case of emergency. Indeed, so popular did skating become that no less than twenty-eight by-laws were introduced to ensure safety, including one banning walking-sticks and another stipulated that gentlemen could only skate on the Ladies' Pond when accompanied by a lady (hence its name).

Elsewhere in the park there were refreshment rooms, on the site of the present Pagoda. Surrounded by a semi-circle of plane trees and by displays of bedding plants, these catered for visitors taking a promenade along the riverside terrace before going to join others at the bandstand for the weekly Sunday concerts. In 1900 the area around the bandstand was enlarged by public demand to permit seating for 1,000 people, with flower beds and pillars of climbing plants screening the audience from the playing fields.

On the pitches close by, cricket continued to be as popular as it had been even before the creation of the park and members of the Cricket Club saw to it that their grounds were preserved throughout the First World War, despite being surrounded by wartime vegetable allotments and military encampments.

In the heyday of the park tennis, too, grew in popularity. Each summer courts were marked out on the grass and fenced in canvas, and eventually hard courts were introduced. Local players were often thrilled to witness matches starring their heroine Mrs Lambert Chambers, the Wimbledon champion between 1919 and 1926. Amongst her youngest fans was at least one member of a foursome which still plays every weekend in the park and are, they claim, so dedicated that only two inches of snow will deter them.

Ironically, whilst the park mellowed and came to fruition in the years leading up to 1914, at the same time it lost some of its pre-eminence as its features were copied elsewhere. However, it was not until the outbreak of the First World War that serious change occurred in this rich and treasured environment.

WAR, PEACE AND WAR AGAIN

The youngest of those who played in Battersea Park as children between the two world wars are now well into middle age. Our memories may be vivid, but are fragmented like clips of old film or even cracked magic-lantern slides. If the factual details of the development of the park between 1918 and 1939 – perhaps to 1945 – are superimposed, two patterns emerge. One is of the deterioration of an elaborately planted Victorian pleasure garden, worn by the pressures of the world outside; the other is of a Garden of Eden.

We know that during both world wars the planting of flower beds and exotic groves was not only abandoned but large areas were dug up for vegetable-growing allotments. The park was used in the defence of London and for the storage of war materials. The gravel carriage drives churned by the lorries of the First World War were widened and macadamised and, by 1919, the look of the park had so coarsened that Viscountess Wolesley wrote in her *Gardens: Their Form and Design* of 'undefined and straggling shrubberies' around 'the

The Battersea Park Pig Club in 1941, during the Second World War.

OPPOSITE: Children at the lakeside, and (ABOVE) the deer enclosure in 1916.

long-grassed, wind-swept plain'. Yet this desolate scene does not accord with the one imprinted upon my own memory a decade later.

To me it was sunlit and flowery; not a playground for the poor of the Battersea slums, which had been a primary purpose, but a Christopher Robin playground, where uniformed nannies sat on benches along the southern shore of the lake, gently rocking their perambulators when their charges became fretful. Can I remember my last day in my pram? I think I can. I am lying on my back in my mobile cot, staring at a blue sky through green leaves slowly passing overhead, and I am thinking that Nanny has said tomorrow all this has got to stop; I will have to get out and walk. I have never quite recovered from the sense of outrage.

The wrought-iron gates and their stone piers inspired by the Arts and Crafts Movement were installed at Sun Gate, as elsewhere, in 1901-2.

We were the children of the flats along what was then called Prince of Wales Road and the houses of Albert Bridge Road. Many of our fathers still called themselves captains or majors – their temporary ranks in the Great War – and, impecunious as they thought themselves, they could usually afford a nanny or a uniformed maid and certainly daily help from the slums.

The slum-dwellers of Battersea were different from those of the East End, for most had no long ancestral history of urban poverty. They were the grandchildren or great-grandchildren of those who had worked in the market gardens of Surrey and were relatively robust as well as quick-witted and

Wooden rowing skiffs, perhaps even the original ones
built by Greaves, in the 1920s.

humorous. They were proud, generous people, too, and I recall no expressed envy of our comfortable lives in the flats; in the little shops of Battersea Park Road our mothers were always 'love' or 'ducks'. For these fine people, for whom hop-picking in Kent was the only possible summer holiday from their mean little streets, the park was a lifeline, not that they could often visit it. But on summer Sundays and Bank Holidays the grass of the playing fields would be invisible for the families sitting there in their thousands, with no space for skipping, let alone cricket.

For them, and us, the greatest treat was a penny cruise round the lake in the

Riverside Refreshment Pavilion, which also sold tobacco and cigars, in the 1910s and (BELOW) on the lake in 1905.

big launch. For special occasions there was a curious motorboat shaped like a swan; the wooden skiffs – probably those built at the Greaves boatyard at Chelsea – were still for hire. The aviaries were, of course, free and at the pheasantry the golden pheasant seemed an impossibly strange and beautiful chimera to city children. Most beguiling of all was to exchange unblinking stares with the owls, sitting on perches in their cave beside the Ladies' Pond, where its remains can still be seen. Then there was the two-storey refreshment house near the river, where the packets of sherbert sucked through black liquorice tubes were banned by middle-class mothers as being impossibly common.

I recall no vandalism or rowdiness in the between-wars park. Partly this was the expected behaviour of a more mannerly age. But it must have had something to do with the platoons of keepers who patrolled its paths in their brown uniforms and trilbies. Most looked as though they had served in the Guards, particularly our genial favourite, Keeper Knight, the ends of whose moustache were waxed into points like horizontal skewers and who wielded his long litter-spike like a rapier.

They were part of the park's swagger. On the now-vanished Rotten Row in the south, lancers sometimes exercised their chargers. Occasionally an open, unescorted landau would sweep along the South Carriage Drive, bearing two nursemaids and two little girls, one an infant. 'Take off your cap, Tommy,' Nanny would command, 'it's the little princesses,' and the Princesses Elizabeth and Margaret Rose would pass by.

They, however, could never experience the two most memorable places in the park: one frightening, the other enchanted. The first was the gaunt Victorian pumping-house lurking at the end of a dark path between high

King George VI and Queen Elizabeth driving through the park to see the flowering shrubs on 17 March 1939.

laurels. We did not know what it pumped or why, but it was sinister – long before its transformation into a friendly art gallery more than half a century later – and we would dare each other to approach its doors in the hope of seeing the grim machinery within and the glint of water beneath its metal floor.

The enchantment was seldom seen. In those days the Cascades were protected by a high, spiked fence, beyond which the waterfalls foamed over their artificial rocks among well-watered flowers and shrubs. Like a small explorer seeking the source of the Nile, I longed to know where the waterfalls came from, so one day I scaled the fence and climbed the wooded hillock. In a grove at the summit I discovered, in a moment of sheer, unbelieving delight, a deep, clear rock pool: a sacred, sensual place and, above all, secret.

Later, of course, the Cascades were allowed to become an adventure playground for stone-throwers and cyclists but now, at the time of writing, there are

In 1922 Field Marshall Lord Plumer unveiled the war memorial (right) sculpted by Eric Kennington

signs that a touch of the old magic may be conjured up again.

Not all memories are sunny. There were the late afternoons in winter when the massed starlings' chorus began in the elms around the lake, the sun set in a dull, red ball through the London murk, and children were hurried home for tea by hissing gas fires.

The end of the First World War had been marked in 1922 by the dedication of a war memorial. This was Eric Kennington's sculpture of three helmeted soldiers, commemorating the 24th Division. If one of them – the one with the broken nose – came to look familiar, it was because the model had been the sculptor's friend Robert Graves, the soldier-poet. The other two were said to be

Wilfred Owen and Sigfried Sassoon.

The start of the Second World War was marked by a less elegant sight: a half-inflated, elephant-grey barrage balloon wallowing at its moorings among the laurel bushes. Then the fields were dug up again for vegetable allotments – more than thirty-two acres of them – and deep-dug for the covered trenches, which became shelters when the bombing began. There was an experimental radio or electronics establishment, and they built a wooden bridge linking the park with Cheyne Walk at the bottom of Royal Hospital Road, as a reserve crossing in case Battersea, Albert or Chelsea bridges were destroyed, striking an echo of Whistler's painting *Old Battersea Bridge.*

In wartime it was not only the park itself which was changed: the sky above was no longer the sheltering bowl of childhood, but somewhere dangerous, where a sudden glimpse of a wheeling gull could jolt the senses – it might have been a banking bomber.

The most dramatic innovation was the siting of an anti-aircraft rocket

FAR LEFT: A poster announcing a procession of military bands during the Second World War.

LEFT: An aerial view of the park looking east, *c.* 1930.

battery on the athletics field and running track. Manned by the Home Guard, this was a parade of concrete plinths topped by steel rails, upon which where mounted the rockets. Fired together with a terrifying 'whoosh' to burst in a flying carpet of high explosive – which, heard for the first time, sent me flying out of and under my bed in Prince of Wales Mansions. Once I had recognised this noise for what it was (that is, friendly), the raids of early 1944 became a nocturnal spectacle of searchlights, bursting shells and the clinking of shell splinters falling in the streets of Battersea.

Peace returned gently. There was an idyllic time when the black-out had been lifted but the street lights had not yet been lit again. The Home Guard had marched away from the rocket battery and the park seemed empty. After dark, I – now in my late teens – would climb the boundary fence and sit with my arm round a girl on a bench overlooking the moonlit lake just below the Cascades and, as it happened, the secret pool.

The Grand Vista in the Festival Pleasure Gardens looking along Fountain Lake towards the river by night, 1951.

FESTIVAL PLEASURE GARDENS AND AFTER

Five years after the end of the Second World War a weary Britain struggled with the consequences of victory and peace. Bread rationing had ceased only two years earlier; austerity prevailed, along with the dull drabness of 'Utility' clothing and furnishings. Pre-fab housing and bomb sites were just around the corner all over London, a grim reminder of the dreadful V1 and V2 bombs which had so indiscriminately plagued the lives of Londoners in the later stages of the war.

Clement Attlee's post-war Labour Government decided that the nation needed a tonic, a celebration of all that was great and good in Britain: a Festival of Britain. Roy Strong described the Festival as 'a celebration of the achievements of Herbert Morrison's Labour Government, making tangible to the masses the Utopia of the Welfare State, the salvation of society seen in terms of universal provision, education and nationalization.'

The Festival fell into two distinct areas: a serious State festival of arts and achievement, and a lighter, 'fun' side for unashamed enjoyment and pleasure. The South Bank accommodated the 'heavy' side, and Battersea Park was to house the Pleasure Gardens.

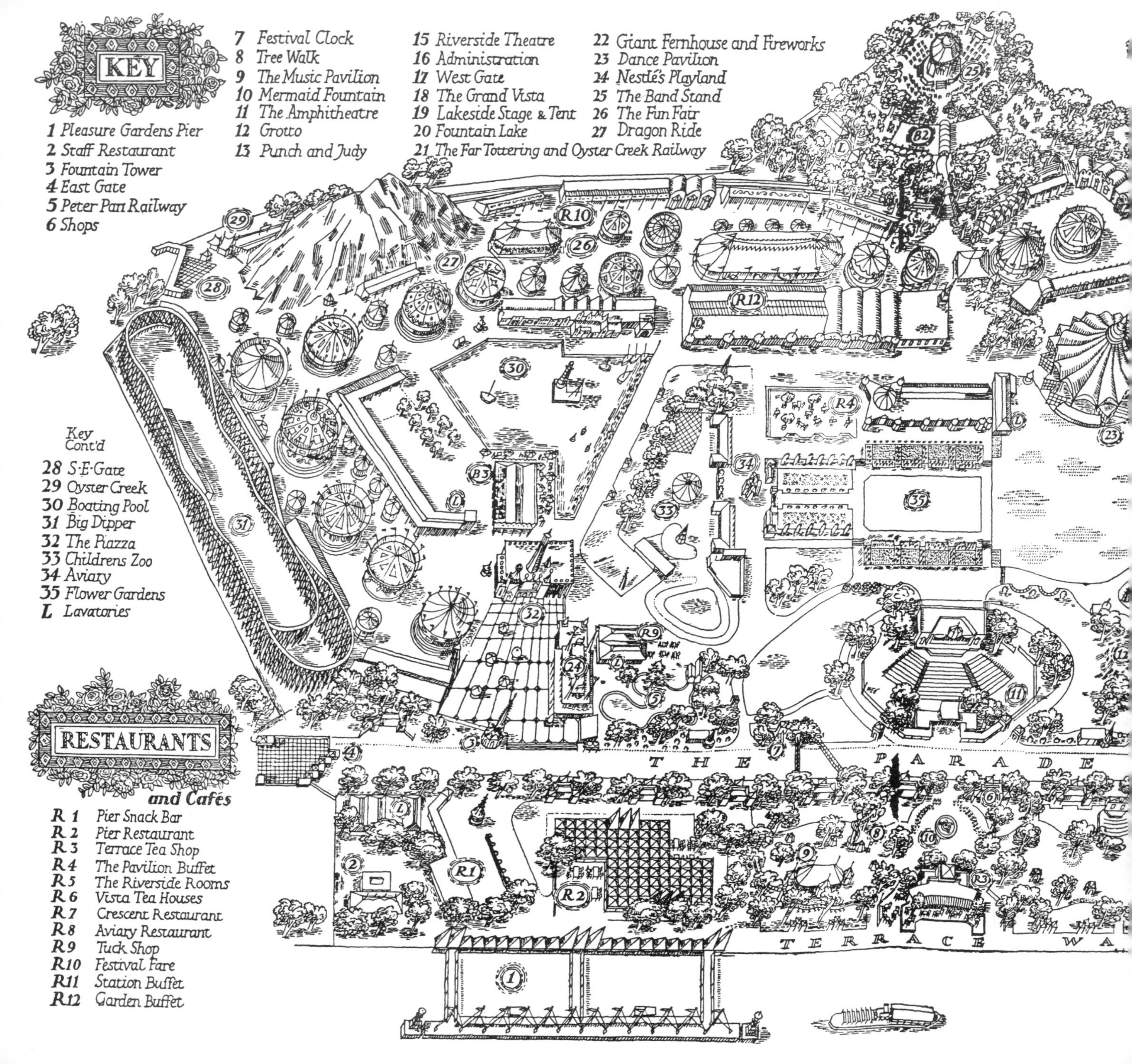

KEY
1 Pleasure Gardens Pier
2 Staff Restaurant
3 Fountain Tower
4 East Gate
5 Peter Pan Railway
6 Shops
7 Festival Clock
8 Tree Walk
9 The Music Pavilion
10 Mermaid Fountain
11 The Amphitheatre
12 Grotto
13 Punch and Judy
15 Riverside Theatre
16 Administration
17 West Gate
18 The Grand Vista
19 Lakeside Stage & Tent
20 Fountain Lake
21 The Far Tottering and Oyster Creek Railway
22 Giant Fernhouse and Fireworks
23 Dance Pavilion
24 Nestlé's Playland
25 The Band Stand
26 The Fun Fair
27 Dragon Ride
Key Cont'd
28 S·E·Gate
29 Oyster Creek
30 Boating Pool
31 Big Dipper
32 The Piazza
33 Childrens Zoo
34 Aviary
35 Flower Gardens
L Lavatories
RESTAURANTS
and Cafés
R 1 Pier Snack Bar
R 2 Pier Restaurant
R 3 Terrace Tea Shop
R 4 The Pavilion Buffet
R 5 The Riverside Rooms
R 6 Vista Tea Houses
R 7 Crescent Restaurant
R 8 Aviary Restaurant
R 9 Tuck Shop
R10 Festival Fare
R11 Station Buffet
R12 Garden Buffet
THE PARADE
TERRACE WA

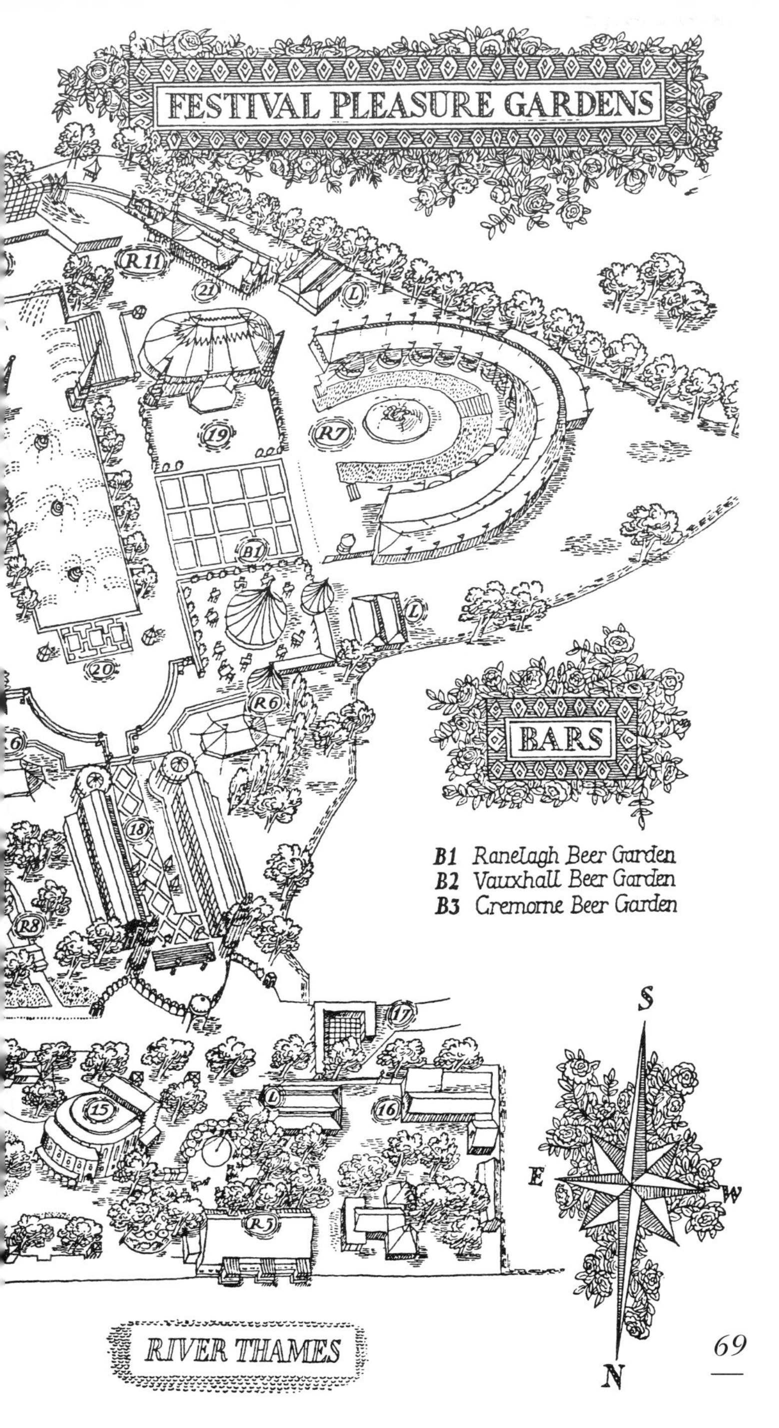

A cartoon-like plan drawn by E. W. Fenton for the official guide to the Festival of Britain Pleasure Gardens, March 1951.

Designer James Gardner took charge of the Battersea Pleasure Gardens project, financed by a Treasury loan of £100,000, later increased to an amazing £570,000, combined with a London County Council loan of £200,000. In an interview twenty-five years later James Gardner recalled: 'Everyone was against the idea, one would think "pleasure" was a rude word. The *Standard* would carry a leader – "Spend the money on St Thomas's Hospital" – it had recently been bombed – and so on.'

The project began to take shape. A thirty-seven-acre site in the park extended from the river back to the central carriageway, and from what is now the Old English Garden in the west to the east carriage drive. There were problems right from the start. James Gardner: 'We found it necessary to cut down a number of the old trees, really large ones, and to prevent a public outcry we would do this late at night, having all the machinery there to cut trees into logs and remove them by morning. I would disguise the stump by placing pots of geraniums on the top and putting a hexagonal seat round it. No one noticed, but early one morning the minister responsible for the parks happened to be walking a dog in Battersea Park and heard the crash as another great tree went down. That, of course, gave another headline for the *Standard*. In fact, the trees we removed were all on their last legs, but people get emotional over trees, quite naturally so.'

The design of the Pleasure Gardens was to embody all that was contemporary and *modern* in Britain; in effect, it was redolent of Scandanivian and Italian designers of the era, Bauhaus and Mies van der Rohe in particular. Five distinct spaces were arranged in the style of the Tivoli Garden in Denmark, through which James Gardner plotted a brilliant circulation system to accommodate the huge numbers expected to attend.

The northern end of the Grand Vista, designed by John Piper and Osbert Lancaster, with a pair of dark red gothic towers. Two shallow rectangular lakes, each with a pair of pyramidal fountains, were flanked by Chinese gothic arcades, all painted in bold colours and gold.

A screen in the shape of the Crystal Palace stood at the southern end of the Grand Vista.

Sir Gerald Barry was the Director General for the Festival of Britain. At the time, Battersea Park was still providing allotment space ('Dig for Victory!'), and it was Barry who decided that Battersea would house the Pleasure Gardens, having at the back of his mind, no doubt, the ancient gardens which had been sited at nearby Vauxhall.

A small army of contemporary designers was assembled: John Piper, Osbert Lancaster, Hans Tisdall, Lewitt-Him, Patrick Gwynne, Bruce Angrave, Rowland Emett and Guy Sheppard were the heavyweight contributors on the list. The whole concept was thought of and designed as a stage set: superficial appearance was all and substance was nothing. Colour was everything. After the dreary, drab war years, almost everything would be red, white and blue, with touches of yellow and gold.

Work on the site continued to be plagued with problems. James Gardner later said, 'We had a lot of labour troubles. The only time all the men were really motivated was when they had a strike meeting. There were a lot of strike meetings. To cap it all, the river flooded and turned the whole area into mud soup. Sad to see the foundation blocks sliding over and tanker trucks pumping up mud to dump it down river. We couldn't drain the site as there was nowhere to drain it to – we literally had to carry the mud away, and that took time.'

Progress was made, though, and bit by bit everything began to fall into place. Although three weeks behind schedule, work on the site was satisfactory enough for James Gardner to take four days away to deal with problems which had cropped up on the South Bank site. He returned to Battersea to find catastrophe. 'The site looked for all the world as though some great monster had walked round vomiting tarmac,' he recalled. 'The contractors had been instructed to lay the stuff over all areas marked as pathways and standings, with the result that the main vista, instead of having a Venetian pavement and shallow steps leading down to the lake, was an undulating landscape of tarmac.'

He agonized over what to do. Courageous, even brass-necked string-pulling paid off and 'I had the joy of seeing Costain's men bulldoze up all the tarmac.'

The centrepiece of the Pleasure Gardens was the vista steps area. Shallow steps led down to pools and fountains, lights, cameo shops and stalls, decorative obelisks and gothic towers, all arranged to please the eye. Young women dressed in seventeenth-century frocks wandered up and down the steps proffering oranges from panniers, gracefully carried at their bent elbows.

ABOVE: Russell Page's Flower Garden with the Pavilion Buffet and the Giant Fern House beyond.
OPPOSITE: The Pleasure Gardens and fairground in 1953.

Copious planting had taken place to give shape and colour to the Festival. While elderly trees and shrubs had been sacrificed, new flowering shrubs took their place: rhododendrons, azaleas, philadelphus, hydrangeas and viburnums. Thousands of bulbs had been planted (20,000 yellow tulips, for example), all of which obligingly flowered in time for the opening of the Festival.

An island of green lawn and flower beds provided an oasis of quiet on the site. Designed by Russell Page, the area sat on a bed of cinders, put down to overcome drainage problems. A free-flowing central part was bordered by formal, raised beds of roses and yew trees. White double stocks were replaced, as the summer continued, with red verbena and foxtailed celosias in orange, scarlet and crimson.

The temporary fairground boating pool and Big Dipper.

To the north of this area lay another famous feature of the Festival, the Schweppes Grotto, designed by Guy Sheppard. Rocks and a waterfall were to be found beyond a rocky entrance, leading to four caves representing the four elements. Children loved this 'secret' place.

The Festival Funfair was located in the north-east corner of the site. This large, tarmac area was perfect for all the traditional funfair attractions and modern rides. The Big Dipper track towered above the fairground, while below the gentler attractions of candy-floss stalls and hoop-la jostled amiably with the Crazy House and the spiral slide.

For teenagers of the day the Rotor was undoubtedly their favourite ride. 'Passengers' filed into the enormous, rubber-lined drum, about twenty at a

In the Riverside Theatre nightly at ten 'Mr Leonard Sachs's Song Saloon' presented old-time music-hall numbers sung by such popular figures as Hattie Jacques, Eleanore Summerfield and Bernard Miles.

time, and stood with their backs to the circular inner wall. Slowly the drum began to rotate, gently picking up speed until it was whirling around so fast that centrifugal force stuck everyone to the side of the drum as firmly as if they had been glued there. Then the floor suddenly fell away, descending about six feet, leaving the passengers stranded half way up the drum like beached whales. It was no coincidence that the boys always lined up opposite the girls, for when the drum began to slow down again, everyone slid slowly down to the floor. Unfortunately for the girls, as they slithered down, their skirts did not . . .

The Pleasure Gardens were originally planned as a six-month event, but it was so popular the authorities decided to extend it for a further six months. Eight million people visited the Pleasure Gardens in the course of the year.

Amongst the branches along the riverside Tree Walk nestled a miniature village, a dragon (seen here) and other beasties.

A scaled-down funfair remained on the site until 1974. Two years earlier, a tragic accident had resulted in the deaths of five children when they were hurled from a faulty ride, and this coloured public opinion on the safety of funfairs in general. The fairground was looking decayed and tatty, and, when it finally closed, no one really mourned its passing.

Various features of the Pleasure Gardens were maintained post 1951: the Tree Walk, the Guinness Clock, the Showboat, the concert pavilion and several cafés. The riverside area was reinstated. Most of the Festival structures were gradually demolished, sometimes not very satisfactorily: crumbling vestiges of the foundations can still be found today.

The Guinness Clock with the Tree Walk in the background and (BELOW) the Showboat on the Pleasure Gardens Pier.

A celebration of the park centenary took place in 1958, and in the following decade new facilities appeared: the adventure playground and its buildings, new changing rooms for sportsmen and women, additional tennis courts and car parks. The Horticulture Therapy Garden for the Disabled appeared in 1972, along with an extremely ugly boathouse.

It was during this period, though, that the park suffered something of a decline. London County Council evolved into the Greater London Council and, under both bodies, there was a lack of enthusiasm (and probably finance) to do anything very much for Battersea Park, although piecemeal improvements were made here and there. The old funfair site became an area for roller-skating and cycling, used from time to time for travelling fairs, circuses and ballets. In 1977, the Queen's Silver Jubilee year, the site was used for an exhibition of British Genius; it has been known as the British Genius Site ever since. For many years there was a large annual Easter Parade of floats round the park, but gradually its popular appeal waned and it was finally discontinued in 1991.

In 1985, amid some controversy, the Peace Pagoda was built. With the abolition of the GLC in 1986, Wandsworth Council took over responsibility for Battersea Park and immediately instigated a brisk programme of improvements. The Victorian bandstand and perimeter railings, sacrificed for their metal content during the Second World War, were replaced. A new athletics track and resurfaced tennis courts were floodlit to provide year-round use; the Children's Zoo was extended and remodelled, and the adventure playground was rebuilt to incorporate new designs and improved safety standards.

A schedule of tree planting was already under way when the Great Storm struck the South of England on the night of 15-16 October 1987. The full

Based on ancient Indian and Japanese Buddhist designs, and donated by Nipponzan Myohoji, the Peace Pagoda celebrated its opening in May 1985.

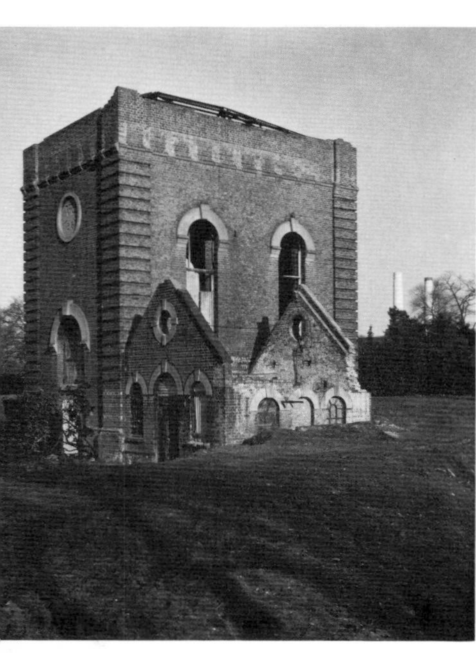

extent of the damage which had occurred on that night was not immediately realized by the park management, and so the public were allowed into the park as usual. Few ventured in, however: power failures, fallen trees and damaged roofs kept most people occupied at home. But those who did visit the park on that bleak Friday morning could only stand and gape at the devastation before them. Huge, lovely old trees lay on their sides, roots sprawling towards the heavens, beside enormous craters from which they had been wrenched by the hurricane-force winds during the night. It was truly the saddest of sights. The ground was littered with branches and boughs torn away by the savage winds.

It seemed, on that day, that Battersea Park could never be the same again: everything seemed to have suffered. Fencing and lamp-posts lay grotesquely twisted on the ground; even the grass looked flattened and defeated. The park was closed for a week while trees were made safe and a general clearing-up operation took place. About 200 trees were lost to the Great Storm in Battersea Park. It was an immense and deeply felt loss to regular visitors, but Wandsworth Council was swift to respond and tree planting was resumed almost immediately.

The new 'jewel in the crown' of the park is the recently refurbished and restored Pump House. A permanent exhibition makes use of video and computers to show the history of the park, while the upper floors provide a classroom and galleries for art exhibitions.

The Victorian Pump House before and after restoration (1992).
Its long-gone steam engine used to pump water from a well,
but the lake was later fed by the Thames.

From the Duke of Wellington's famous duel to the present day, Battersea Park has represented rapidly changing times. Today, Queen Mary and the little Princesses could not drive informally through the park in an open carriage with any safety. The technology of warfare has advanced to a stage where a world war lasting for six years is inconceivable, and the idea of a London park being made over to allotments during that time to provide food for the local population is almost laughable.

Brown-suited park keepers who, with a threatened clip round the ear, inspired both fear and respect from errant children caught, perhaps, walking on the grass, have been replaced by the Parks' Police. These brave men and women have to cope with bomb scares, muggings and drug abusers, as well as the more mundane theft from cars and drivers who flout speed restrictions. Police vehicles and personal radios are anathema to some, but they help maintain Battersea Park as a much-loved area of greenery and peace for Londoners and visitors alike. The squawk of a police radio may be irritating, but it serves as a reminder of the times in which we live – a far cry from the days when a young lad was fined five shillings for kicking a ball in the park on a Sunday.